MEET THE SWIMMING REPTILES

by Rebecca Donnelly
illustrated by Alan Brown

GRASSHOPPER

Tools for Parents & Teachers

Grasshopper Books enhance imagination and introduce the earliest readers to fiction with fun storylines and illustrations. The easy-to-read text supports early reading experiences with repetitive sentence patterns and sight words.

Before Reading

- Discuss the cover illustration. What do they see?

- Look at the glossary together. Discuss the words.

Read the Book

- Read the book to the child, or have him or her read independently.

- "Walk" through the book and look at the illustrations. What is happening in the story?

After Reading

- Prompt the child to think more. Ask: Marine reptiles are good swimmers. What body parts do they have that help them swim? How are they similar to fish? How are they different?

Grasshopper Books are published by Jump!
5357 Penn Avenue South
Minneapolis, MN 55419
www.jumplibrary.com

Library of Congress Cataloging-in-Publication Data

Names: Donnelly, Rebecca, author.
Brown, Alan, illustrator.
Title: Meet the swimming reptiles / Rebecca Donnelly; illustrated by Alan Brown.
Description: Minneapolis, MN: Jump!, Inc., [2022]
Series: Meet the dinosaurs!: when reptiles ruled
Includes index.
Audience: Ages 7-10
Identifiers: LCCN 2021037987 (print)
LCCN 2021037988 (ebook)
ISBN 9781636906201 (hardcover)
ISBN 9781636906218 (paperback)
ISBN 9781636906225 (ebook)
Subjects: LCSH: Marine reptiles, Fossil–Juvenile literature. Dinosaurs–Juvenile literature.
Classification: LCC QE861.5.D6848 2022 (print)
LCC QE861.5 (ebook)
DDC 567.9/37–dc23
LC record available at https://lccn.loc.gov/2021037987
LC ebook record available at https://lccn.loc.gov/2021037988

Editor: Eliza Leahy
Direction and Layout: Anna Peterson
Illustrator: Alan Brown

Printed in the United States of America at Corporate Graphics in North Mankato, Minnesota.

Table of Contents

Life in the Water

Come swim with me! I'm Piper the Plesiosaurus. I look like a dinosaur, but I'm a marine reptile. I live in the water, but I come to the surface to breathe.

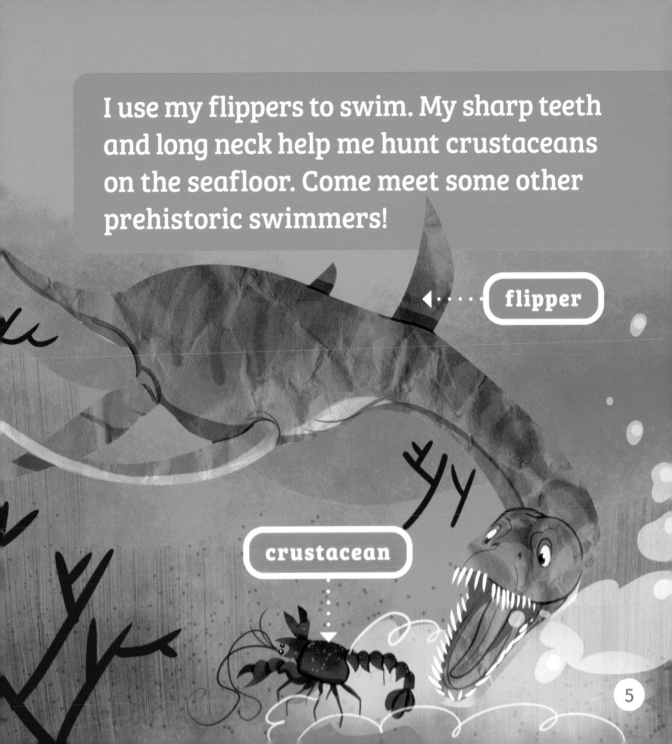

I use my flippers to swim. My sharp teeth and long neck help me hunt crustaceans on the seafloor. Come meet some other prehistoric swimmers!

flipper

crustacean

Hi, I'm Eli the Elasmosaurus. I'm 46 feet (14 meters) long. My neck is half the length of my body! It has 72 bones in it.

Watch me hunt this group of fish. I reach down with my long neck. *Snap!*

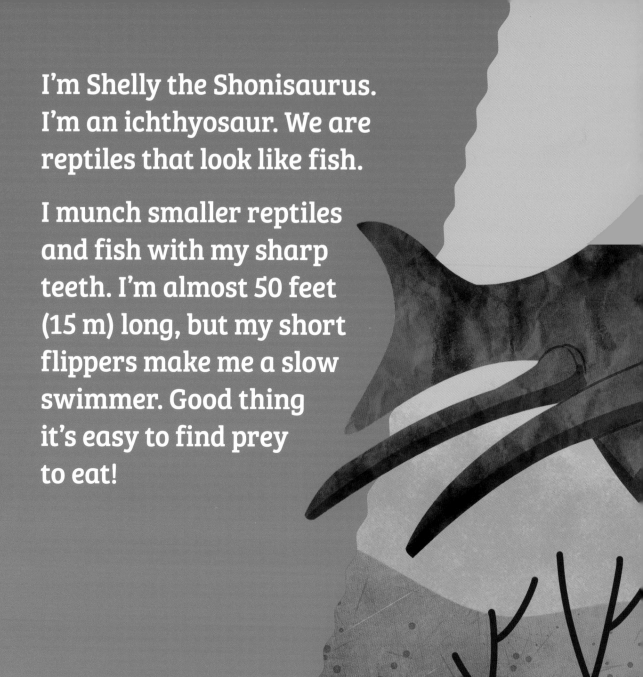

I'm Shelly the Shonisaurus. I'm an ichthyosaur. We are reptiles that look like fish.

I munch smaller reptiles and fish with my sharp teeth. I'm almost 50 feet (15 m) long, but my short flippers make me a slow swimmer. Good thing it's easy to find prey to eat!

I'm Milton the Mixosaurus. Take a look at my crew!

At just over 3 feet (0.9 m) long, we're not very big. We each have four flippers and a long tail. These help us move through the water. We love squid!

squid

shellfish

I'm Parker the Placodus. I hunt my dinner along the coast. My front teeth point forward to pick up yummy shellfish. I crush the shells with my back teeth and eat the soft insides.

When a predator comes for me, I go on land! It can't reach me here!

You'd better swim the
other way if you see me!
I'm Drake the Dakosaurus.
I'm related to crocodiles.
Can you see the similarities?

I use my huge, sharp
teeth to take bites out
of my prey. If my meal
is small enough,
I swallow it whole!

prey

I'm Corey the Concavispina. I'm not as scary as Drake. Unless you're a jellyfish!

I have small teeth, so I eat soft foods. To swim, I move my body and my long tail from side to side. *Swish!*

tail

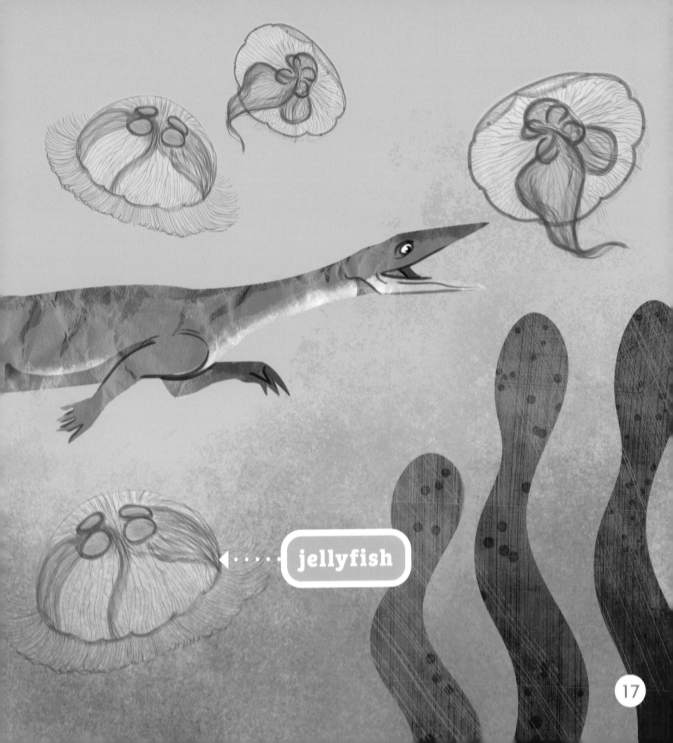

jellyfish

I'm Nora the Nothosaurus. I live on land, but I hunt in the sea. My webbed feet help me swim.

webbed foot

I eat fish and other marine reptiles. There's one!

These other swimmers are shrimps compared to me! I'm Marie the Mosasaurus. I'm 56 feet (17 m) long, and I'm fierce! I'll eat anything, even other marine reptiles.

We're all extinct now, but we used to swim in every ocean. There's lunch! Gotta go!

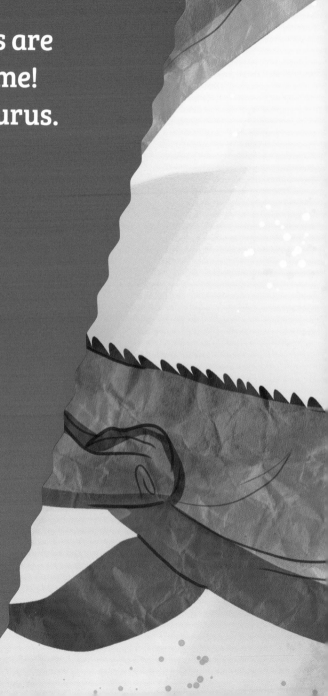

Timeline

Dinosaurs lived millions of years ago.
Take a look at when the dinosaurs
in this book lived!

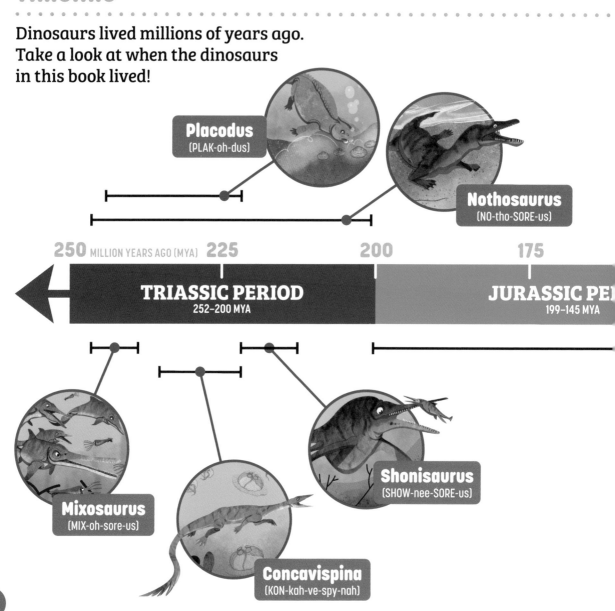

Placodus
(PLAK-oh-dus)

Nothosaurus
(NO-tho-SORE-us)

250 MILLION YEARS AGO (MYA) 225 200 175

← **TRIASSIC PERIOD**
252–200 MYA

JURASSIC PE
199–145 MYA

Mixosaurus
(MIX-oh-sore-us)

Concavispina
(KON-kah-ve-spy-nah)

Shonisaurus
(SHOW-nee-SORE-us)

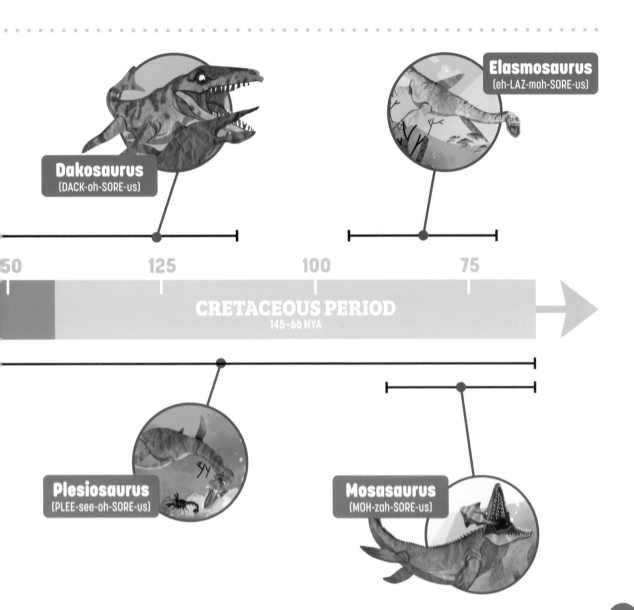

Dakosaurus
(DACK-oh-SORE-us)

Elasmosaurus
(eh-LAZ-moh-SORE-us)

50   125   100   75

CRETACEOUS PERIOD
145–66 MYA

Plesiosaurus
(PLEE-see-oh-SORE-us)

Mosasaurus
(MOH-zah-SORE-us)

Glossary

crustaceans: Sea creatures that have outer skeletons, such as crabs, lobsters, and shrimp.

extinct: No longer found alive and known about only through fossils or history.

marine reptile: An animal that breathed air and lived in water but was not a true dinosaur.

predator: An animal that hunts other animals for food.

prehistoric: Belonging to a time before history was recorded in written form.

prey: Animals that are hunted by other animals for food.

shellfish: Creatures with shells that live in water, such as crabs, oysters, and mussels.

Index

To Learn More

FACT SURFER

Finding more information is as easy as 1, 2, 3.

❶ Go to www.factsurfer.com

❷ Enter "**meettheswimmingreptiles**" into the search box.

❸ Choose your book to see a list of websites.